Mrs. Addicott.

Mrs. Addicott.

British Library Cataloguing in Publication Data

Hobson, Wendy
  Easter book.
  1. Easter – For children
  I. Title   II. Nest-James, Rhian
  394.2'68283

  ISBN 0-356-16809-3
  ISBN 0-356-16810-7 Pbk

EASTER

A STORY AND ACTIVITY BOOK

Written by

Wendy Hobson

Illustrated by

Rhian Nest James

Consultant:

Beryl Goodland

Macdonald

CONTENTS

THE REBIRTH OF SPRING

For thousands of years, Easter has been a time for celebration all round the world. The name 'Easter' comes from 'Eostre', the ancient goddess of spring and the dawn.

Try to imagine what winter must have been like all those years ago. It was cold, with no prospect of a warm house or a hot bath. There was no electricity to lighten the long evenings. Food was in short supply. Is it surprising that people celebrated the coming of spring?

Many religious festivals also occur in spring, for example the Jewish Passover. When the Israelites — the ancestors of the Jews — were slaves in Egypt the Pharaoh refused to free them. So God sent an Angel of Death to 'pass over' their city. The eldest son in every Egyptian family died, but the Israelites escaped.

The date for Easter is different every year. It falls on the first Sunday after the first full moon on or after the spring equinox (21 March). Confused? Try this: Easter is between 21 March and 25 April!

Since Jesus' death and resurrection happened at Passover, Easter has become more important than ever. Even in the southern hemisphere — where it signals the onset of winter — the people share many of the same traditions.

Jesus began his teaching when he was about thirty years old and his ministry lasted only a few years. The core of his teaching was love for God, and for one another — a simple message, which Jesus explained in simple terms. It has influenced the lives of millions of people the world over.

THE STORY OF EASTER

Palm Sunday

It was the Sunday before Passover. In the city of Jerusalem excitement was mounting as the Jews looked forward to their celebrations in memory of the time when God had freed them from slavery in Egypt. The Romans, who governed Judea at that time, had brought in extra troops in case of trouble.

Jesus and his disciples were on their way to the city, but the disciples were unhappy and confused. Jesus was their teacher and friend. He had told them that he would be arrested, tortured and killed, but three days later would return to life. How could it be true? It did not make sense.

Just outside Jerusalem, Jesus sent two of his disciples to the edge of a small village. 'You will find a donkey tied next to its mother,' he told them. 'Untie it and bring it to me. If anyone asks what you are doing, just say, "Our Master needs it."'

The disciples brought the donkey to Jesus and laid their cloaks on its back. Jesus climbed on and joined the procession of pilgrims travelling towards Jerusalem.

When they saw Jesus, the people became more excited. He had been called 'the Messiah', and their holy books said that such a man would free them from oppression. Had he arrived at last to raise his army against their Roman rulers? Waving palm branches in the air, they threw them down in Jesus' path, shouting, 'God bless the man who comes in the name of the Lord!'

Teaching in the Temple

The crowd followed Jesus to the temple court where traders and moneylenders often set up their stalls. Overturning their tables, Jesus drove them out, shouting,

'You are turning my house of prayer into a thieves' den.'

For the next few days, Jesus taught in the temple, and people flocked to listen to him. The blind and crippled came to him and he healed them with a touch.

The chief priests watched with mounting anger and jealousy. Jesus was telling the people to love one another and not to be concerned with power or wealth. They were both rich and powerful and wanted to stay that way. They had to find a way to stop him without upsetting the crowds.

They hatched a plan to trick Jesus so that they could have him arrested as a trouble-maker. But he saw through their plans and avoided the trap.

'They are the leaders of the Church, and you must do as they say,' Jesus told his disciples, 'but not as they do. They say they serve God, but they serve themselves, for they are only interested in money and power, not in other people.'

Angered by their failure, the priests decided to wait until the Passover festival. Their chance came sooner than they expected. Judas Iscariot, one of Jesus' disciples, offered to betray his friend for thirty pieces of silver.

The Feast of the Passover

On the day of the Passover, Jesus sent Peter and John into the city. He told them they would meet a man carrying a pitcher of water.

'Follow him home and ask him where the Master will celebrate Passover with his disciples. Prepare the feast in the upstairs room he will show you.'

They did as he said and prepared the feast.

That evening, the disciples were taken aback when Jesus began to wash their feet. This was a job for a servant!

'You must serve others, as I do,' Jesus told them.

During the meal, Jesus became very sad. He broke the bread and passed it to his friends, and poured wine for them.

'This is the last time I shall eat with you,' he told them. 'So you must take bread and drink wine as a way of remembering me when I have gone, for I will leave you very soon. And it is one of you who will betray me.'

'I will never go against you,' Peter assured him.

'Before the cock crows,' Jesus told him sadly, 'you will deny that you know me three times.'

The Arrest

After their meal, Jesus and his disciples went to a nearby garden, called Gethsemane. Jesus walked away to be alone, and kneeling on the ground, he prayed in sorrow.

'If it is part of your plan,' he prayed, 'please save me from what is about to happen.' Then he went back to his friends, for he felt lonely and needed their companionship. But they had all fallen asleep.

'Could you not stay awake for an hour?' he asked; although he knew that they were tired and unhappy. Three times he went away to pray alone, and each time he returned to find them asleep. Finally, he woke them, saying, 'Wake up. My enemies are on their way.'

As he spoke, a crowd of armed men came into the garden. Judas was with them, and he greeted Jesus with a kiss.

Both knew this was a pre-arranged signal. The guards seized Jesus. Furious, Peter drew his sword and sliced off a man's ear.

'Put down your sword,' Jesus told Peter, then he touched the man's ear and healed him. 'If I wanted to be rescued, I could call on armies of angels. Everything must happen as it has been prophesied.

'But why have you come to arrest me with swords and sticks as though I were a robber?' he asked the soldiers. 'You could have arrested me at any time in the temple.'

They had no answer, but roughly took Jesus away. The disciples fled in terror in case they were seized as well.

The High Priest

Jesus was taken before Caiaphas, the high priest. Peter and John followed at a safe distance and waited outside.

Caiaphas was determined to convict Jesus of a crime deserving the death penalty. He knew that he must appear to do everything legally or risk Jesus' followers turning against him. He arranged for many people to testify against Jesus. But as they were all lying, they all told different stories. Jesus would say nothing to defend himself, even though they insulted and beat him. Finally, frustrated and angry, Caiaphas demanded,

'Are you the Messiah?'

'Those are your words, not mine,' Jesus replied calmly. 'But I tell you that from now on the Son of Man will sit at the right hand of God.'

'He is claiming to be sent from God!' the priests cried furiously. 'He has condemned himself!'

Meanwhile, Peter had been recognized as a friend of Jesus, but he denied it. Twice more, people challenged him, but each time Peter said that he did not know Jesus. Then he heard the cock crow. He left and cried bitterly for abandoning his friend.

When Judas saw that the priests wanted Jesus dead, he regretted his actions. He tried to return his money, but they refused to take it. In desperation, he hurled the coins down in the temple. Then he ran away and hanged himself.

Pontius Pilate

Jesus was led in chains before the Roman governor, Pontius Pilate. Only he could sentence a man to death.

'This man is a traitor,' the priests claimed. 'He says he is our king when everyone knows that you rule here.'

'Are you the King of the Jews?' Pilate asked Jesus.

'You say that I am,' was all Jesus would reply. Pilate was amazed that he would say nothing to defend himself. He realized that Jesus was innocent.

'He has done nothing to deserve death,' he told them.

It was the custom at Passover to release a prisoner, so Pilate offered to free Jesus. Seeing their plans about to fail, the priests incited the crowd to shout for Barabbas, a rioter and murderer.

Pilate had a problem. It was the custom to free the man chosen by the people; so what was he to do with Jesus? He could not find him guilty of any crimes.

Again, the priests stirred up the people, and they yelled, 'Crucify him!' This was the most cruel death they could demand, reserved for the worst criminals and slaves.

The crowd was dangerously excited. If he did not give them what they wanted, Pilate feared they would riot. He dared not risk it. He made a show of washing his hands.

'My hands are clean of this man's blood. It is you who have decided to kill him.' Releasing Barabbas, he had Jesus whipped and handed him over to be crucified.

The Crucifixion

The soldiers stripped Jesus and dressed him in a scarlet cape and a crown of thorns because the Jews had called him a king. They laughed at him, spat on him and beat him. Then they dressed him in his own clothes and led him to a hill called Golgotha, which means 'the place of the skull'. Jesus was so weak that the soldiers forced a man called Simon to carry his cross.

When they arrived at Golgotha, the soldiers stripped Jesus and gambled for his clothes. He refused the drugged wine they offered him. Then they nailed him to the cross, fixing the sign of his crime above his head.

'This is Jesus, the King of the Jews.'

And though Jesus was in terrible pain, he asked God to forgive his murderers. But the soldiers and the priests laughed at him.

'If you are the Son of God,' they mocked, 'come down from the cross and save yourself.' Even one of the two thieves who were crucified with him joined in their taunts. But the other thief stopped him. Jesus could see that this man was sorry for the evil things he had done.

'We will meet in Heaven,' he told him.

From midday until three o'clock, the skies stayed dark as though it were the middle of the night. Then Jesus cried,

'Father, I place my spirit in your hands. It is finished,' and he died. At that moment the curtain of the temple was ripped in two, and the earth shook.

The people who were watching felt deeply sad.

'This man really was the Son of God,' they said.

The Burial

That evening, a man called Joseph from Arimathea went to Pontius Pilate. Joseph was rich, but he was a good man and he was a follower of Jesus. He knew that the bodies of criminals who had been crucified were thrown into a mass grave and did not want this to happen to Jesus. So he plucked up the courage to ask Pilate if he could take the body away. Pilate agreed.

Helped by a friend called Nicodemus, Joseph took the body and wrapped it in clean linen. Then he laid it in his own tomb, which had never been used before. A huge stone was rolled across the entrance. Mary Magdalene and Jesus' mother watched from a distance.

The next day was the Sabbath. The women wanted to buy perfumes and spices to embalm the body, but as no one could work on the Sabbath, they could do nothing.

The chief priests had work to do, however. They knew that the scriptures said that Jesus would be raised on the third day. If this happened, they would be proved wrong and more people would follow Jesus than before. They went to Pilate and asked him to guard the tomb.

'Otherwise,' they argued, 'someone will come and steal the body and claim that Jesus has been raised from the dead.'

Pilate agreed and sent soldiers to watch over it.

Resurrection

At daybreak the next day, Mary Magdalene went to the tomb only to discover that the huge stone had been rolled away. She rushed off to find Simon Peter and John and gasped out the news to them.

They ran back to find the tomb empty, and only the linen wrappings inside. The disciples walked sadly home. But Mary sat outside the tomb and cried. Then she saw two angels sitting at the head and feet of where the body had been.

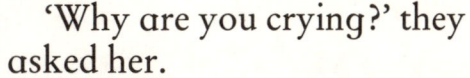

'Why are you crying?' they asked her.

'Because I don't know where they have taken my master's body,' she replied. Then she turned away from them and saw a stranger outside. She thought he must be the gardener.

'Why are you crying?' he asked. 'Who are you looking for?'

'If you know where they have taken the man who was buried here, please tell me,' she begged. Then he said,

'Mary,' and she recognized at once that he was Jesus. He told her to go and tell his friends that he was alive.

She hurried off to find the disciples hiding in a locked room because they were afraid the priests might kill them too. They felt lonely and sad because they had lost their best friend. Mary's news was astonishing; could it really be true?

Spreading the Good News

That evening, Jesus appeared in the room. At first, the disciples thought they must be seeing a ghost. But Jesus talked to them and showed them the wounds in his hands and feet. When he explained that everything had happened exactly as God had promised it would, they finally believed that he had come back to life. From fear and sadness, their mood changed to joy.

'I will always be with you,' Jesus told them. 'You have seen me and believe in me. Now it is your job to tell others my messages of God's love and forgiveness. Just as I have come to life, everyone who believes in God has the chance of eternal life.'

Later, Jesus blessed the disciples and was taken up into heaven. The disciples could hardly contain their joy. They went to the temple to thank God for his message of love and forgiveness. Death need no longer frighten them. If they believed and trusted in God, they could follow Jesus through death to a new life.

CELEBRATIONS AROUND THE WORLD

Easter is celebrated the world over. Ancient customs have mixed with Christian ones until they are sometimes hard to separate. Some spring celebrations relate to other religions.

Christian Traditions

In the story of Jesus, you can see the start of many customs. The cross on which Jesus died was taken as the symbol of Christianity. Holy Communion is a reminder of the Last Supper, and the fact that Jesus died to save others. The palm crosses given on Palm Sunday recall Jesus' triumphant entry into Jerusalem.

Do you sometimes have a new outfit for Easter? This dates from when Christians were baptised in new robes on Easter Saturday. Others wore new clothes to remind them of their own baptism.

Maundy Thursday – a Day for Giving

The Thursday of the Last Supper is named after an old word meaning 'I give'. Many churches and special charities give money or food to the elderly, and the Pope washes the feet of twelve priests on that day. Many years ago, the British monarch used to wash the feet of the poor, but this custom has now died out.

Instead, the Queen gives specially-minted 'Maundy money' to some elderly people, one for each year of her age.

Processions and Parades

These are very much a part of Easter, like the Palm Sunday procession in Jerusalem. Some German priests ride to church on a donkey on Palm Sunday.

Processions in Easter week are solemn. On Good Friday, people in Jerusalem follow Jesus' path to Golgotha. In Spain, people walk barefoot after huge statues of Jesus and Mary.

Easter Sunday shows and parades are joyful, like the famous Royal Easter Show in Sydney, Australia, and the New York Easter parade.

Unusual Festivities

Statues of the gods are carried through the streets at the Indian festival of Holi, which happens at Easter. It celebrates the love of the Hindu god Krishna for Radha. People light bonfires and eat special foods. Guests' foreheads are marked with red powder, and people throw red powder and coloured water over each other.

Bonfires are lit in Sweden at Easter to ward off witches! The children have great fun dressing up.

A spring flower festival is held on the Buddha's birthday in Japan. They sprinkle scented tea round the temples and decorate them with flowers.

The Easter Rabbit

Hare-hunting used to be part of the ancient festivals of Eostre. Somehow, over the years, the hare has been replaced by a rabbit.

The rabbit is popular because he brings the eggs. Like Father Christmas, he travels a long way, hiding eggs in gardens from Australia to Holland for children to discover on Easter Sunday. Some German children make nests of moss for him to fill.

French children hunt for eggs hidden by the church bells. The bells are silent from Thursday until Easter Sunday, and it is said that they go to Rome to fetch the Easter eggs.

Egg Games

There are all sorts of traditional games played with eggs, such as tossing them higher in the air than anyone else, racing with an egg on a spoon, and knocking eggs together to try to break your opponent's egg without cracking your own. The most famous egg game is played by rolling eggs down a slope to see whose egg can reach the bottom first without being cracked or broken. They play this on the American White House lawns every year.

Easter Chicks

From the eggs, of course, hatch the chicks! Bright yellow – the colour of spring – they provide another reminder of new life coming from what is apparently dead.

A CLUTCH OF EGGS

Eggs have always been a symbol of new life, so they are especially appropriate at Easter. The first decorated eggs were painted red in memory of Christ's blood. Now they are painted all different colours, and also made from wood or metal. The most famous precious eggs were made from gold and jewels by a man named Fabergé, for the Tsar of Russia.

Coloured Eggs

Try these different ways of dyeing eggs for an extra special Easter Sunday breakfast.

For a brown marble egg: wrap the egg in brown onion skins and tie it in a piece of an old pair of tights.

For a green egg: wrap the egg in spinach leaves and tie it in a piece of an old pair of tights.

For a brown egg: add two teabags to the water.

For a red egg: add a raw beetroot to the water.

For other colours: add food dyes to the water.

Boil the egg for 15 minutes. Allow to cool. Then polish the warm egg with a little vegetable oil on kitchen paper.

Blowing Eggs

Leave the egg in a warm room for a few hours. Prick the narrow end with a pin and make a larger hole in the other end. Place your fingers over both holes and shake hard. Hold the egg over a bowl and blow through the small hole. Dry.

Painting and Decorating Eggs

Paint hard-boiled or blown eggs with any non-toxic paint. Varnish blown eggs, or rub cooking oil on ones for breakfast.

Try patterns or pictures of animals, flowers or palms.

Draw a design with a wax crayon, then paint over it.

Use masking tape to make a stencil pattern, then paint the egg and remove the tape.

Paste patterns on your egg using tiny beads, cut paper, wool or braid.

Papier Mâché Eggs

This is fun but very messy, so be prepared! You need flour and water paste, a balloon, newspaper, paints and varnish.

Ask an adult to help you make the paste. Put one cup of plain flour in a saucepan with one heaped teaspoonful of salt. Slowly add one cup of cold water and stir. Bring to the boil and simmer for one minute. Cool.

Blow up the balloon. Soak strips of newspaper in the paste and wrap them around the balloon. Leave to dry for two days. Cut in half, paint and varnish the egg, or use braid and beads to decorate it. Line it with a doily and put presents or eggs inside.

23

EASTER GREETINGS

Friends will appreciate a home-made card at Easter.

Easter Rabbit

1   Fold a long piece of card into two.

2   Paint the Easter rabbit on the front with his ears bent over along the top fold.

3   Cut round the edge of the rabbit and the space between his ears.

Chattering Chick

1   Fold a piece of paper in half lengthways and make a 4cm cut a quarter of the way up the fold.

2   Fold the paper back from the fold to make two triangles.

3   Flatten the paper, then fold into four, widthways, then lengthways with the cut inside.

4   Pull apart the centre points of the slit so that it folds into the open beak of a giant chick.

5   Paint the chick's face and a springtime scene on the front.

24

DECORATIONS AND GIFTS

Here are some simple things to make to decorate your home at Easter, or to give as gifts to your family and friends.

German Willow Twigs

Arrange some willow, or other branches, in a vase. In Sweden, they put birch twigs in water to blossom on Easter Sunday. Use ribbon or wool to hang decorated or chocolate eggs, eggshell baskets, pretzels and little chicks on to the twigs.

To hang a blown egg, tie a used match to a piece of cotton and put the match into the hole in the egg. Pull gently on the cotton and the match will turn sideways.

Easter Chicks

Two yellow cotton wool balls, glue, paper and a felt tip pen make a super Easter chick.

Fluff out one ball for a body and stick it to the head. Draw on eyes, or stick on two tiny beads. Cut a diamond shape of paper, fold it in half and stick it on for a beak. Stick on two triangles of paper for feet.

25

Eggshell Baskets

You need half an eggshell, washed and dried, glue, paint, varnish and ribbon.

Paint and varnish the shell. Glue a piece of ribbon around the rim and another from top to bottom and tied into a handle. Fill with sugar eggs, sweets or a cotton wool chick.

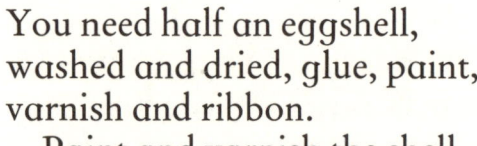

Spring Flowers

For a paper daffodil, find a pipe cleaner, an egg box, a card from the lid of a coffee jar and some paints.

Cut five petal shapes in the card circle, and one cup section from the egg box. Paint them yellow. Thread the pipe cleaner through the cup and the card and twist it to fix it firmly.

Serve a Special Breakfast

Get up early and lay the breakfast table with napkins and perhaps some spring flowers. You can serve decorated eggs with hot toast and coffee – or whatever your family likes.

Where Did You Get That Hat?

For a simple hat, cut a large triangle of card, then make a slit along the bottom edge. Paint it or decorate it with pictures cut from old magazines, streamers of tissue or crepe paper and crumpled dots of tissue paper.

Instead of cutting a triangle, you could make your bonnet in the shape of a rabbit, a chick or a huge egg.

For something more special, use an old hat as a base. Your mum may have some scraps of material to cut into petals and sew on, or see what you can do with egg boxes, crepe paper or tubes from a kitchen roll cut into spirals. The only limit is your imagination!

27

EASTER FEASTS

After the hardship of winter, spring has always been a time for special feasts.

The Passover

This meal reminds the Jews of their escape from Egypt.

Lamb for the lamb's blood they smeared on their houses to protect them from the Angel of Death.

Eggs for their new life.

Unleavened bread because they had no time to wait for their bread to rise.

Bowls of salt water and bitter herbs for the unhappiness of slavery.

Cups of wine for God's promises to free them.

Forty Days Fasting During Lent

Before Easter begins there is a 'fast' called Lent. A fast is a time when people do not eat much. Lent is kept in memory of the 40 days and nights that Jesus spent in the wilderness without food. Early Christians looked forward to feasts after Lent. Hens had continued to lay, but the eggs had not been eaten, so there were always lots at Easter.

Hot Cross Buns

The Ancient Greeks ate spiced cakes at their festivals – you can make Hot Cross Buns. Buns baked early on Good Friday morning are supposed never to go mouldy. Some were strung across the kitchen ceiling, then grated into medicines. Sailors carried a stale bun to ward off shipwrecks!

Chocolate Nests

100g Margarine
50g Soft brown sugar
2 Rounded tablespoons Golden Syrup
2 Rounded dessertspoons Cocoa
100g All Bran or Shredded Wheat
Sugar eggs and marzipan

1   Slowly melt the margarine,
     sugar and syrup.
     Stir in the cocoa.

2   Crush the Shredded Wheat
     lightly.
     Mix the cereal into the
     chocolate mixture.
     Allow to cool slightly.

3   Shape into 10 small nests.
     Leave on a greased baking tray
     in a cool place to set.

4   Fill with eggs.
     Roll two balls of
     marzipan for a chick.
     Use cloves for eyes and
     coloured marzipan
     for a beak.

Simnel Cake

This fruit cake is decorated with 11 balls of marzipan to represent the 11 disciples, without Judas.

150g Butter
150g Soft brown sugar
3 Eggs, lightly beaten
200g Self-raising flour
2.5ml Cinnamon

2.5ml Nutmeg
100g Sultanas
350g Currants
50g Ground almonds
450g Almond paste

1 Cream the butter and sugar until light and fluffy. Beat in the eggs, a little at a time.

2 Fold in the flour and spices. Stir in the fruit and ground almonds.

3 Put half the mixture in a greased, lined 18cm cake tin.

4 Roll out the almond paste and cut into two 18cm circles. Roll the trimmings into 11 balls.

5 Put one marzipan circle on the cake mixture in the tin, and cover with the rest of the mixture.

6 Preheat the oven to 180°C/350°F/Gas mark 4 and bake for about 2½ hours.

7 When cool, put the second circle of almond paste on the top and place the 11 balls round the edge.

A MACDONALD BOOK

Printed in Great Britain by
Purnell Book Production Ltd
A member of BPCC plc

Macdonald & Co (Publishers) Ltd
66–73 Shoe Lane
London EC4P 4AB

A member of Maxwell Pergamon
Publishing Corporation plc